Melody

A play

Deirdre Kinahan

Samuel French — London
www.samuelfrench-london.co.uk

Please see page iv for further copyright information

MELODY

First performed by Tall Tales Theatre Co. at the Temple Bar Information Centre and the LAB in Dublin, 2005, with the following cast:

Mr Kane	Steve Blount
Kathleen	Maureen Collender

Directed by Veronica Coburn

CHARACTERS

Kathleen, a receptionist, 40s
Mr Kane, an IT professional, 40s

SYNOPSIS OF SCENES

The action takes place in and around Dublin

Time — the present

AUTHOR'S NOTE

Although the original play was set in Dublin, it is possible to change the location to suit individual productions.

NOTE ON THE ACTING EDITION

When one character starts speaking before the other has finished the point of interruption is marked /.

e.g.

Mr Kane You don't mind taking the late lunch do you, Mary? I've … I've a bit of a /date.

Kathleen Date — the 23rd. Yes, two suites to be charged to the card. You have the details ——

For my Dad, who no doubt kissed my Mam on
Brighton Square.
For Gráinne, who met her man on a park bench.
And for my man, Gary.

Each scene is titled and announced by a design device like a changing menu or clicking calendar. The first is LUNCH

It is a sunny day. Kathleen is sitting on a park bench eating nicely cut sandwiches. She is in her forties. She opens a juice carton with a squeeze and the juice spills everywhere. She looks around, embarrassed. She returns to her sandwiches

Mr Kane, also well into his forties, arrives and takes up the seat beside her

Kathleen looks nervous. Mr Kane moves up an inch. She moves up along the bench. He settles, she goes to move again and almost falls off the edge. He reaches to catch her and they both sit. She is mortified. She resumes eating her sandwiches and looks out front

Mr Kane They look nice. (*By way of explanation*) The sandwiches.
Kathleen Oh yes, ham and cheese.
Mr Kane Lovely.
Kathleen (*after a pause*) Would you like one?
Mr Kane Don't mind if I do.

He takes one and they both eat, smiling. There is a pause

Isn't it a lovely day?
Kathleen Lovely.
Mr Kane It's been a nice spell.
Kathleen Oh it has — lovely … really mmn … lovely.
Mr Kane Yes.

Kathleen Would you like a mini éclair?

Mr Kane Well, aren't you well organized?

Kathleen (*chuffed*) Oh well, one has to be. Particularly nowadays with everything running so fast … life you know — whoooosh — it flies, doesn't it?

Mr Kane It does. Though you seem very relaxed.

Kathleen Do I?

Mr Kane Yes. I saw you sitting here, amidst all the madness and I thought — now there is a special lady, a sea of calm.

Kathleen Really, did you? Me … a sea of calm?

Mr Kane Yes.

Kathleen Well you'd want to see me at the office.

Mr Kane Whooosh!

Kathleen (*laughing*) Exactly.

Mr Kane (*after a pause*) Are you here for the music?

Kathleen Hmm?

Mr Kane The music, here in the park ... the summer concerts!

Kathleen Oh of course, yes I am actually. Do you like them too?

Mr Kane Oh, yes.

Kathleen They add a little magic to the day I always say.

Mr Kane Oh, they do though, don't they though?

Kathleen (*after a pause*) It was such a lovely morning, I thought I'll get the concert in the park and take in a little vitamin D.

Mr Kane Oh yes, enjoy it while it lasts.

Kathleen Absolutely …

They both laugh. There is a pause

I always think the sun brings out the best in people. Gives you a little lift.

Mr Kane Oh, yes.

Kathleen The girls in work were all out basking in it when I left, splashing on the "Hawaiian Tropic".

Mr Kane Ahh.

Kathleen I don't take a colour at all though I'm afraid. I enjoy the warmth of a shady nook.

Mr Kane Ahh. (*He pauses*) Do you work nearby then?
Kathleen I do, not far at all. And you?
Mr Kane Just across the road … in the Department of the Marine.
Kathleen Oh, lovely. (*She pauses*) I love the sea.
Mr Kane Really.

There is a pause

Kathleen It's a good selection today I think, I should have the flyer here. (*She takes a flyer from her pocket*) Yes, Wagner, Mahler, Strauss and Brahms.
Mr Kane Ahh, you know your music then!
Kathleen Oh not at all, no — just a novice.
Mr Kane I doubt that.
Kathleen No, really … I'm not really interested in the names, the composers and all that — no I just love the notes, the musical notes, melodies … beautiful sounds floating out. (*Embarassed*) I haven't got a clue really. I'm sure I sound daft even talking about it.
Mr Kane Not at all. You listen with your heart.
Kathleen Oh, isn't that nice … with my heart. (*She pauses*) I suppose I do. And you, Mr ah ——
Mr Kane Kane, William Kane. Pleased to meet you.
Kathleen Likewise. Kathleen Hill.
Mr Kane Kathleen … lovely.
Kathleen (*after a pause; thrilled*) So do you go to concerts often then, Mr Kane?
Mr Kane Oh, yes.

There is a pause, followed by an air of expectation. There is another pause

Kathleen And do you do a lot of sailing?
Mr Kane (*bemused*) Sailing?
Kathleen Yes.
Mr Kane No.
Kathleen Oh.
Mr Kane Oh, because I'm in the Department …

Kathleen Yes. I'm sorry, how silly … I realize now that ——
Mr Kane No, I work in IT.

Kathleen doesn't have a clue what this means

Kathleen Oh, lovely.
Mr Kane I work with computers. Not a sailor, I'm afraid.
Kathleen (*acutely embarrassed*) Of course.

There is a pause

Mr Kane Do you use computers?
Kathleen Computers … Oh I do, now, yes, I got trained.
Mr Kane Excellent.
Kathleen I had to put in a system, you see, there was no system at all at the office before I arrived.
Mr Kane So you installed it.
Kathleen (*lost*) Installed?
Mr Kane The computer system.
Kathleen Oh lord no, I just organized the books and things —— appointments. I set up a system for calls, booking the rooms and the like.
Mr Kane Ah, secretarial. You're in secretarial?
Kathleen Yes, sort of. I set up the system but then Justin decided we should transfer it all to computer, move out of the dark ages as he said, so I did the course, you see. ELC, CL thingy.
Mr Kane Ahh.
Kathleen Yes. I'm a dab hand at it now. Can manage almost everything I need to do.
Mr Kane Well if you ever need a hand, just give me a call. I solve problems, computer problems at the department. I could help you out if there was a crisis.
Kathleen Oh really? Very good … well that's very kind of you, Mr Kane, thank you.
Mr Kane Most welcome. (*Handing her a business card*) My card.
Kathleen (*impressed*) Oh.

There is a pause. Kathleen handles the card, smiles, carefully puts it into her handbag and smiles again

Mr Kane (*after a pause*) I wonder …
Kathleen Yes
Mr Kane Well … well I wonder could I tempt you to another luncheon on Thursday?
Kathleen Oh.
Mr Kane I believe it's Puccini.
Kathleen Puccini, oh wonderful.
Mr Kane Yes.
Kathleen Yes.
Mr Kane Well?
Kathleen Well …
Mr Kane Would you like to …
Kathleen Oh yes, of course, of course — Puccini. I think that would be lovely, Mr Kane.
Mr Kane William.
Kathleen William, yes … of course.

A waltz by Strauss fades in

They both remain sitting, looking pleased

SCENE 2

WORK appears on the title device

This is a split scene. Both Kathleen and Mr Kane are in their respective work places and their monologues should intertwine, overlapping on the repeated words and then perhaps growing in speed and intensity until a shrill bell rings, marking lunch for both of them so they can escape to each other and their bench

A phone rings in Kathleen's office

Kathleen (*picking up the phone*) Sex Connections, can I help you? …

Oh, hallo Mr Dwyer, how are you? … Good. Feeling better after that
nasty cold? … Well I'm delighted. … It's really not a good idea to go
swimming at that hour you know, it is far too cold at night. … Yes,
but perhaps you could try some other pursuits. … Well I know one
client enjoys tennis. … Naked, yes. … No, we don't have a special
relation with an LTC, the client has his own court I believe. … True,
might be difficult, I'm just suggesting there may be alternatives to
swimming. … Right. So, you'd like to make an appointment for
Monica is it? … Um, hmmn, /in an hour? …

Mr Kane   (*on the phone*) In an hour. … Yes. … The server should
probably definitely be almost back up in an hour, sir. … Yes, I know
it's very diff —— … Yes, I know it's inconven —— … Two hours
work. It wasn't saved? … No, I'm not sure that it can be recov ——
… No. Of course. … Unreliable. Absolutely. … Our incompetence.
… Yes. … No I'm not being smart. I sympathize. Really. … No, it
certainly isn't personal sir. … I just, I need —— … Well you see I
can't fix it while —— … Of course. Right away, as soon as I have it
working I'll come directly to your /office ——

The caller has evidently hung up

Kathleen   (*on the phone*) Office here, Monica. … How are you? …
Listen, can you fit Mr Dwyer in, in an hour? … Yes, at the Forty Foot.
… I know, there's just no talking to him. … Do you need swimwear?
… Excellent. Now I see he required goggles last time out, so inform
me of any extras, Monica, and I'll add them to the invoice. … He
what? … A snorkel! … Well you put your foot down Monica, you
know our policy on out-of-parlour appointments — the girl knows
best! … Don't do anything you're not comfortable with, dear. …
Right, so Monica, /thank you.

Mr Kane   (*in conversation with an imagined colleague; beleaguered*)
"Thank you" — It's only a small word, isn't it Mary, but not much
chance of hearing it in this game. Jesus. But they're a vulnerable
breed, the end user. Stressed. Always stressed. I feel like a punching
bag in here some days, I don't mind telling you. If we can't get your
man's document back, there'll be hell to /pay.

Kathleen (*to a customer at the parlour*) Pay prior to the appointment, sir. Thank you, that's excellent. Straight through the double door. ... No, no, no that's not a camera — part of the alarm system. ... Not at all, we place great emphasis on confidentiality here at the parlour. It comes at a cost of course but then cost is rarely an issue /nowadays ...

Mr Kane Nowadays there is no patience, is there, Mary? Years ago when we started off, there was great wonder, wasn't there? A great kind of gobsmackery at what might be achieved by computers, but now it's all "not quick enough", "unreliable", "laborious". Everyone wants the work done /yesterday.

Kathleen (*on a direct line to her boss's office*) Yesterday's receipts are totalled, Justin. All the girls are booked out for the day and I'm about to organize two for the Tullamore weekend /service.

Mr Kane Service that computer, Mary, and I'll make us a cuppa. Now where's /that newspaper?

Kathleen That newspaper man was on the phone again, Justin. He keeps asking to interview the girls. I ran him. Such a persistent little ——

Mr Kane (*stirring his tea*) Shite. The server is down for the day! And what am I supposed to tell your man?

Mr Kane's phone rings and he raises his eyes to the sky. He picks it up and hangs it up

He almost cried the last time, Mary, I'm not kidding ya. "Effing shite", he says, "effing culchie, effing thick, effing useless —— "

Kathleen's phone rings as she tries to get ready to leave

Kathleen Shite! (*Into the phone*) Sex Connection, can I —— ... Oh Alex thanks for calling back. ... Can you do the Tullamore run for me this weekend? ... Great. ... Yes, there'll be two of you going down. I'll book the transport and the hotel and get back to /you.

Mr Kane You don't mind taking the late lunch do you, Mary? I've ... I've a bit of a /date.

Kathleen Date — the 23rd. Yes, two suites to be charged to the card. You have the /details ——

Mr Kane (*as if joking with Mary*) Details, what do you mean details?

Kathleen I need to book two rail /tickets ——

Mr Kane (*laughing*) Ticket, I said you're a ticket.

A shrill ringing sound stops them in their tracks. Kathleen hangs up

Mr Kane } (*together*) Ah, lunch.
Kathleen }

   Mr Kane exits

Kathleen is about to leave when the phone rings again. She pauses, then lets it go to the answer machine

Kathleen's voice (*on answering machine*) Welcome to Sex Connection, I am sorry there is no one to take your call at the moment, just leave a message and we'll get back to you.

There are some breathy, heaving sighs in the background. After a "beep" Mr Kane's voice can be heard. He starts humming a well-known tune then speaks

Mr Kane's voice (*on answering machine*) Ah, Miss Officientus. Mr Amadeus here. (*Humming a little of his tune again*) Hope you are well. I would like to make an appointment for Monica please, Saturday, usual time, Wynn's Hotel.

Kathleen mouthes Wynn's Hotel as she is very familiar with Mr Amadeus

   Thank you, dear Miss Officientus, talk again next week. (*He hums another bum-di-bum-di-bum*)

   Kathleen finishes powdering her nose and leaves, having heard the message

Black-out

SCENE 3

THE DATE appears on the title device

Mr Kane enters. He carries his sandwiches. He sits and looks about for Kathleen. He looks straight out to the audience and waits. He looks about for Kathleen. He opens his bag, takes a peek then closes it. He looks about. He looks out. He waits. He takes out a messy sandwich and takes a bite

Kathleen arrives, late and a little fussed. She is behind the bench, she sees him and stops, thrilled. She adjusts her hair and skirt, then approaches the bench. He is oblivious, takes another bite and is all mayonnaise and stuffed mouth as she arrives and he stands up to greet her. There is an awkward shuffle as she takes a seat and he nearly chokes in an effort to greet her

Kathleen I'm so sorry I'm late. I simply couldn't get out of the office.

Mr Kane Not at all, not at all.

Kathleen Have I missed Puccini?

Mr Kane No, no, he must have heard you'd been delayed.

Kathleen Ah. (*Laughing*) Such a glorious day.

Mr Kane Indeed. Indeed. (*He pauses*) I'm afraid I started! I wasn't too sure whether you'd be coming.

Kathleen Oh and you were perfectly right to, the lunch break brief as it is. (*Producing her own box of tricks*) Now, I hope I wasn't a little presumptuous, but as you suggested the concert, Mr Kane, I thought I'd take the liberty on lunch.

Mr Kane William, please, William. How kind!

Kathleen I hope you don't mind.

Mr Kane Mind? I am delighted and very sensible of you considering I ate half of your supplies on Tuesday!

Kathleen (*laughing*) Well, I thought a little ravioli in honour of the Italian prince!

Mr Kane Ah, Mangiare Musica!

Kathleen (*excited*) Yes.

Mr Kane Magnifico.

Kathleen Focaccia, with a little pesto.

Mr Kane Aha.

Kathleen Olive salad … aaaand a little tiramisu for afters.

Mr Kane Miss Hill, I, I am honoured.

Kathleen Tchhh, Kathleen.

Mr Kane No, honestly. This is incredibly generous.

Kathleen Well it's a bit of a laugh.

She hands him his little tub of ravioli and starts into her own. She has even remembered to bring plastic forks. They eat and smile at each other

Mr Kane Delicimo.

The music starts

Kathleen Oh and now the music.

Mr Kane Perfect.

They both react throughout to the music as they eat, but less perhaps as they get into conversation

   Are you looking forward to the weekend then, Kathleen?

Kathleen Oh, yes. And you?

Mr Kane Oh, yes.

There is a pause. They continue to eat and smile

Kathleen And if the weather holds …

Mr Kane Oh, absolutely.

Kathleen I'm sure I'll spend much of it in the garden.

Mr Kane Beautiful, beautiful.

She hands him the salad and he gets caught with a bitter olive

Kathleen Do you garden, William?

Mr Kane No, not really. Mine is a little terraced house — "Sandy-mount".

Kathleen Oh, how lovely.

Mr Kane Just a yard. A few sorrowful looking pots and the recycle bin.

Kathleen Well there is a lot of work in a garden.

Mr Kane Indeed.

Kathleen But the flowers are worth it. Such colour!

Mr Kane And where is this colourful garden?

Kathleen Templeogue.

Mr Kane Ah.

Kathleen The Terenure end …

Mr Kane Excellent. (*He pauses*) And have you family with you in Templeogue?

Kathleen No, no. My husband is deceased.

Mr Kane Oh, I'm sorry.

Kathleen Three years now.

Mr Kane I'm dreadfully sorry.

Kathleen Oh no, he's in a better place … Dear Raymond.

Mr Kane Of course.

Kathleen He was ill for a long time.

Mr Kane Oh no.

Kathleen Oh yes. MS.

Mr Kane Oh dear.

Kathleen We had it all our married life.

Mr Kane Oh I'm sorry.

Kathleen (*after a pause*) A dreadful condition.

Mr Kane No …

Kathleen It was like a breakdown of all the capacities really.

Mr Kane Terrible …

Kathleen Poor Raymond. He was lovely.

Kathleen is getting quite upset and Mr Kane is in a lather

Mr Kane I'm sure … that's terrible — I — I …

Kathleen But we had our good times despite everything.

Mr Kane Of course.

Kathleen You have to make the best of things, don't you, Mr Kane?

Mr Kane Oh you do though, don't you though.

There is an awkward pause

Kathleen And you?
Mr Kane Me?
Kathleen Have you family?
Mr Kane No, no.
Kathleen No?
Mr Kane The bachelor boy …
Kathleen (*smiling*) I see. (*Pause*) I do have my mother in Dublin.
Mr Kane Ah, well that's a comfort.
Kathleen Yes.
Mr Kane And does she stay in Templeogue?
Kathleen No. She's in Rathgar.
Mr Kane Well that's not far.
Kathleen In a nursing home.
Mr Kane Oh.
Kathleen She suffers from Alzheimer's.
Mr Kane Oh no.
Kathleen Three years now.
Mr Kane Terrible.
Kathleen Yes.
Mr Kane An affliction.
Kathleen Gosh, you must think I'm a jinx.
Mr Kane No, no.
Kathleen You must.
Mr Kane You're just unfortunate.
Kathleen I suppose.
Mr Kane Well that's life isn't it? When you reach a certain age …
Kathleen Age?
Mr Kane I mean as one moves on in life.
Kathleen Moves on, oh yes.
Mr Kane Yes.
Kathleen Moves on. I'll go visit Mother on Sunday — we always do Sundays.
Mr Kane Ah, well that's lovely.
Kathleen It is.

Another awkward pause

And your parents, William, are they still with us?
Mr Kane Oh yes, well the mother's still in Navan.
Kathleen Navan … I wondered about your accent.
Mr Kane Oh Navan town, through and through.
Kathleen And is your father?
Mr Kane No, no, he's gone the past few years.
Kathleen I'm sorry.
Mr Kane The mother has her sister with her. Annie. They still keep the shop.
Kathleen Shop?
Mr Kane Ah, 'tis only a small affair.
Kathleen In Navan?
Mr Kane Yes.
Kathleen Aren't they marvellous?
Mr Kane I suppose. Ah, sure they enjoy the chat and that.
Kathleen Of course. And what do they sell?
Mr Kane It's a class of a hardware, you know, mousetraps, milk, bulbs, screws, this and that.
Kathleen Terrific to keep it all going.
Mr Kane I suppose. Something to get up in the morning for.
Kathleen Yes.
Mr Kane I'll just try a bit of that foc-eh-foc stuff.
Kathleen Of course … Because that's the stuff of life, isn't it, William? The doing.
Mr Kane Well it is I suppose. Wouldn't you go daft if you were at nothing?
Kathleen Oh certainly.

They both laugh. Mr Kane hums a few bars of the music as he chews his focaccia

Ah. It's *La Bohème*.
Mr Kane A favourite of mine.
Kathleen Really? Mine too!

Mr Kane There's nothing like the music to lift you!

Kathleen I'm sorry I got a little upset earlier.

Mr Kane Oh no, no, Kathleen. There's a little bit of sadness in all of
us.

Kathleen I suppose. (*She pauses*) Could I tempt you to the
tiramisu?

Mr Kane Well I thought you'd never ask!

They smile and continue to enjoy themselves

The music gets louder as the Lights fade

SCENE 4

HOPE appears on the title device

*This is another split scene. Kathleen and Mr Kane are standing in their
respective homes. They talk directly to the audience*

Kathleen I was telling Mother about William. She was pink she was so
pleased. Mother's in quite a nice place now. Gone are the days of the
terrible anxiety — thank God. She seems to have just surrendered to
the confusion so I never know who I'll be when I visit. It all depends
on the memory she's occupying. I could be an old school friend, her
sister, her mother … but today, today was special. I started to tell her
my news as I always do but something about William tickled her, she
became very excited and it was as if we were both transported. We
were young friends sharing love stories and she started to tell me about
Dad — at least I think it was Dad — her first kiss on Brighton Square.
Isn't that lovely to know? To know about your own mother. The world
will be never the same again, she said, it's so much brighter.

Mr Kane I was telling Mammy about Kathleen. I think she was a bit
startled by the news. Well it's not that often I visit I suppose and I'd
never tell her much about my life — outside of work like. I'd never
talk about women. But Kathleen's different. I wanted Mammy to
know, you know, but she didn't, she didn't really react, either way.

Well I suppose it's a lot to take in on one visit and she is eighty-two she is. Eighty-two. "How can a man hit forty-six and never have a girlfriend to speak of?" That's all the auld aunt had to say. I was kind of sorry then I said anything. We were never much for that kind of talk in the house, I suppose. Any kind of talk.

Kathleen I sometimes can't quite believe in William. He is such a gem. What an honour to know two good men in one life. Not that I'm taking William for granted … there's been no major "movement" if I can put it like that … but I do believe we're hitting the right note! (*She laughs a little*)

Mr Kane I think I might invite Kathleen down for a few days. Ignore that auld one and let her meet Mammy for herself. We could see the sites. Kathleen's a cultured woman, she'd enjoy Meath. I'd enjoy it myself.

Kathleen I was thinking of inviting William over. Take us beyond the park! I could cook beef. A good fillet seared on a hot pan … with asparagus maybe. (*Tossing her head*) Greek salad tossed, drizzled then with a fine oil. (*Getting carried away and running her fingers over her face*) I'd do a seafood starter and sorbet, summer berries just to tempt. (*A smiling sigh*) Oh and tomorrow is "Music from the Orient" …

She starts to sway and waltzes to the classical music, William joins her in her daydream and they waltz around the stage. She is lost in her fantasy while he delivers the following monologue as they continue dancing together

Mr Kane I don't quite know myself how I got here. It's been a lonely road, I suppose, but to be honest it only seems that way now I've met Kate. I think I was happy enough with the single life until now … The job took a lot of my time and the courses at night. But I've always been a sociable man. I'd go to the dogs with the lads from work, I like a match and a pint … but I dunno, as others settled I … I dunno. I suppose I got left. And I never really felt that until now … now when I'm not left at all! Now, when I'm almost there, at the cusp, falling … falling … well, I dunno. Everything just seems so much brighter now.

They dance for a while

SCENE 5

CLICK appears on the title device

Kathleen and Mr Kane arrive at the bench simultaneously with a real pep in their step

There is a funny sequence as he motions for her to sit and she does a "no after you" type motion. Eventually they sit isimultaneously, looking terribly pleased

Music plays and it has a classical Eastern ring

Mr Kane Well, here we are.

Kathleen Yes.

Mr Kane In our little spot.

Kathleen I saw someone sit here yesterday evening when I walked through for my bus and I almost told him to get up!

Mr Kane You never.

Kathleen Almost!

Mr Kane And what have we today, then?

Kathleen (*producing some food*) Hummus and cherry tomato.

Mr Kane Hummus!

Kathleen A little Eastern promise.

Mr Kane Ya divil ya!

Kathleen Accompanied by a citrus noodle salad! (*Producing chopsticks and two little bowls of salad*) One must be in flavour with the music!

Mr Kane Putting it up to me, you are.

Kathleen Now, now Mr Kane you always produce an exquisite filling.

Mr Kane Straight from "O'Briens". I'll never match your home-made gastronomics. (*Indicating the chopsticks*) Now how do ya manage these?

Kathleen You need to get a good grip lower down.
Mr Kane Right so.

Mr Kane can't get anything into his mouth, gets into a sweat and eventually knocks the entire contents all over himself. Kathleen hurriedly rescues him and gives him the houmous and pitta bread which he eats with great relief

    Well the sandwich is marvellous.
Kathleen Mmmn.
Mr Kane Hummus. Hummmm—us.

Mr Kane hums the tune being played and Kathleen smiles, moving her head to the music. They both enjoy their food

    I've always been fierce fond of a Friday!
Kathleen Mmm. I like Mondays too — heralding in the week.
Mr Kane Hum, hum, hum, hum.
Kathleen All the days melted in to one when I was at home with Raymond. It's nice to have structure … routine.
Mr Kane I suppose.
Kathleen Have you always worked, William?
Mr Kane Since the day I left the brothers in Navan.
Kathleen Did you go straight to the Civil Service?
Mr Kane I did. Haven't even moved department.
Kathleen Really?
Mr Kane Just not the adventurous type, I suppose!

There is a sequence where the couple take up a series of poses, as if in picture frames. They pose in time with the sound of a camera clicking, denoting that someone is photographing them at lunch. They break out of the poses

    Jesus, what's that?
Kathleen What?
Mr Kane I thought there was a flash!
Kathleen Where?
Mr Kane (*pointing ahead*) There.

Kathleen I didn't see anything.
Mr Kane Oh.

There is a pause

   I was wondering …
Kathleen Yes?
Mr Kane I was thinking …
Kathleen Yes?
Mr Kane Would you like to spend a few days down with me?
Kathleen Oh.
Mr Kane In Navan.
Kathleen Oh.
Mr Kane You could meet the mother and … it's a grand town …
Kathleen Yes.
Mr Kane Restaurants, races … and fierce big on heritage.
Kathleen Oh!
Mr Kane They've done a great job on Newgrange.
Kathleen Have they?
Mr Kane Interpretive centre, toilets, there's a bus to it and all, there
   is — and sure Tara's only up the road.
Kathleen Why, yes.
Mr Kane High seat of Ireland.
Kathleen Yes.
Mr Kane I was thinking it might be nice to stay the few days you see,
   I haven't done that in years.
Kathleen No.
Mr Kane No?
Kathleen No, I mean you've haven't done that in years?
Mr Kane Oh.
Kathleen No?
Mr Kane No.
Kathleen No, I mean I'd really love to.

There is another series of clicks and photographic poses

Mr Kane What's that fella at?

Kathleen (*her moment ruined*) What?

Mr Kane See him over there, that young fella in the bushes? He has a camera.

Kathleen Where?

Mr Kane Look at him, facing this way.

Kathleen Who?

Mr Kane That young fella — look.

Kathleen In the rhododendron?

Mr Kane Jesus, he's running off now.

Kathleen Who?

Mr Kane He was taking our photo. He took our photo!

Kathleen He couldn't.

Mr Kane He did.

Kathleen But sure what on earth for?

There is the sound of a camera rewinding. The two are frozen in a pose

Scene 6

EXPOSURE appears on the title device

These monologues are directed to the audience

Kathleen Trouble always treads silently, doesn't it? Like an illness … spreading its poisonous tentacles with precision and patience, always making sure it has a good grip before piercing you with the pain. Then it's unstoppable. Shattering. Do you know, I couldn't care less if it wasn't for William. I don't feel any shame in what I do — we do — at Sex Connection. And there is no one to pay me a blind bit of notice bar Mother and she — well! It simply doesn't concern her. Her world is beyond all this "vice".   I think that's what they called it, yes.

Kathleen lifts the newspaper, displaying the front page picture of herself and William at lunch under the headline "VICE QUEEN PICNICS IN THE PARK"

Can you believe it? And a picture of me and William enjoying our crudité.

Mr Kane Mrs Kelly was all of a dither. Blessed herself when I walked into the shop. Dropped the euro on the floor and all she did. Sure I didn't know what was up (*He pauses*) And then I saw it, first page of the supplement — a picture of me and Kate. God, but it's strange to look in at yourself amidst the print. And it's a nice photo really if you could take the story out. Right out. Poor Kate. She's no vice queen but she is the voice on the telephone — Miss Officientus — how did I not hear it and we at lunch? (*Perplexed*) God, I wonder … is this the end of it all now?

Kathleen It's some jumped up journalist doing an exposé. "Irish Sex Industry Thrives" — and he has me as one of Dublin's top madams. Fool. God, but who's the fool? William. Oh, William, what will they say in the department? And in Navan? I mean, dear God, it's in all the Sundays! (*She pauses*) His mother! The woman's eighty-two. She's eighty-two! They'll have to shut up shop for a week. What must William think? Good, sweet, William. I'll never see him again, sure how on earth could I explain? Consort! Pervert! That's what they imply. Oh merciful God, poor William … and he at his Sunday roast!

Mr Kane I'll have to try and see her. Be sure to get things straight. Templeogue — sure that's all I have is Templeogue. She's sure to be in a state. Isn't he a right bastard with his Vice Queen? I should have had him when I had the chance. I'll try the office again.

Kathleen I haven't heard a peep from the office. I mean, will we all be arrested? Dear God, I'm so afraid! So afraid that that's the end of it all — the light, the lunch ——

Mr Kane …The park. I'll go straight over and explain the lot — Monica … and … and … and …

Kathleen He'll never …

Mr Kane I'll tell her everything.

Kathleen Not now.

Mr Kane Yes.

Kathleen No.

Kathleen is distressed. Mr Kane is upbeat and determined

They both exit

Scene 7

MISSING YOU *appears on the title device*

This is a physical sequence. Mr Kane arrives at the bench with brown paper bag containing lunch for two. He waits. Kathleen never arrives. Mr Kane doesn't eat. He waits. He leaves

Kathleen arrives, just missing him. She has a cheap sandwich in cellophane. She opens it, looks at the filling and sighs

Kathleen Oh William!

She exits in great distress

Mr Kane arrives with a picnic basket and red rose. He sits, looks, waits and eventually exits

Kathleen arrives, just missing him. She has a kebab and throws herself on the bench in melodramatic manner. She cries, sits up, goes to eat the kebab, then makes as if to vomit. She exits

Mr Kane arrives with two Chinese bamboo baskets complete with chopsticks. He waits and eventually leaves

Kathleen arrives, just missing him. She has a box of cholocate bars and eats one. She is totally dishevelled as Mr Kane enters and sees her. He has a sandwich

Scene 8

MELODY appears on the title device

Mr Kane Hallo, Kathleen.
Kathleen (*drying her eyes and putting the chocolate away; faltering*) William!
Mr Kane Do you mind if I ...

Kathleen Oh no, no no, of course not!
Mr Kane Thanks.
Kathleen (*after a pause*) William, I … I …
Mr Kane Have you had lunch?
Kathleen Um … no.
Mr Kane Would you do me the honour?
Kathleen Oh, oh yes thank you.

Mr Kane only has one sandwich now as he thought he'd lost her. He gives her his sandwich

Mr Kane Ham and cheese.
Kathleen Lovely.

There is a pause

Mr Kane I was afraid I'd lost you.
Kathleen Oh, William.
Mr Kane I need to explain.
Kathleen No, I need to explain.
Mr Kane No.
Kathleen I'm so terribly sorry. I had no idea about the article … I …
Mr Kane You are a beautiful woman, Kathleen.
Kathleen Oh.
Mr Kane And it's a privilege to spend any time with you at all.
Kathleen Oh, William, but after all I've put you through. I … It must have been such a shock. You see it's just my job, I take the calls …
I —
Mr Kane … Miss Officientus.

Kathleen stops dead in her tracks

Kathleen (*looking at him*) What?
Mr Kane Miss Officientus.

He hums his tune, very low

Kathleen Mr Amadeus?
Mr Kane Yes.

Kathleen You're Amadeus?
Mr Kane Yes.
Kathleen Oh my God!
Mr Kane Kathleen!
Kathleen And did you know all along?
Mr Kane No, not until I read the article.

Pause

Kathleen But all this time we …
Mr Kane Yes.
Kathleen Oh.
Mr Kane Sure, how were we to know?
Kathleen I suppose.
Mr Kane Do you mind?
Kathleen What?
Mr Kane Well, my … my being Amadeus?
Mr Kane Oh! No, not really. Should I?
Mr Kane Well …
Kathleen I'm not a "Vice Queen".
Mr Kane No.

*Kathleen sings the first line of "Stand By Your Man" by Tammy Wynette.
Mr Kane then sings the second line and Kathleen sings the first few
words of the third line*

Kathleen (*speaking*) You like to sing?
Mr Kane Yes.
Kathleen Would you like to sing to me, Mr Kane?
Mr Kane William.
Kathleen (*smiling*) William.
Mr Kane It would be an honour.

*Mr Kane steadies himself and then sings "It's You, It's You, It's You"
by Joe Dolan*

They kiss at a suitable juncture

THE END appears on the title device

FURNITURE AND PROPERTY LIST

SCENE 1

On stage: Scene title device: LUNCH
Park bench
Lunchbox containing neatly cut sandwiches, juice carton, mini
  éclairs (for **Kathleen**)

Personal: **Mr Kane**: business card
Kathleen: flyer

SCENE 2

On stage: Scene title device: WORK
Telephone, answering machine (in **Kathleen**'s office)
Telephone (in **Mr Kane**'s office)

Off stage: **Kathleen**: make-up

SCENE 3

On stage: Scene title device: THE DATE
Park bench
Bag containing sandwiches with mayonnaise dressing (for
Mr Kane)

Off stage: Lunchbox containing two tubs of ravioli, foccacia, pesto,
  olive salad, tiramisu, plastic forks (**Kathleen**)

SCENE 4

On stage: Scene title device: HOPE

SCENE 5

On stage: Scene title device: CLICK
              Park bench

Off stage: Lunchbox containing hummus and cherry tomato, two bowls of
              citrus noodle salad, chopsticks, pitta bread (**Kathleen**)

SCENE 6

On stage: Scene title device: EXPOSURE
              Newspaper for **Kathleen**

SCENE 7

On stage: Scene title device: MISSING YOU
              Park bench

Off stage: Brown paper bag containing lunch for two (**Mr Kane**)
              Sandwich in cellophane (**Kathleen**)
              Picnic basket, red rose (**Mr Kane**)
              Kebab (**Kathleen**)
              Two Chinese bamboo baskets, chopsticks (**Mr Kane**)
              Box of chocolate bars (**Kathleen**)
              Ham and cheese sandwich (**Mr Kane**)

SCENE 8

On stage: Scene title device: MELODY
              Park bench

Off stage: Scene title device: THE END (**Stage Management**)

LIGHTING PLOT

To open: General exterior lighting

Cue 1:   They both remain sitting, looking pleased   (Page 5)
             Lights fade to black-out

SCENE 2

To open: General interior lighting

Cue 2:   **Kathleen** finishes powdering her nose and leaves   (Page 8)
             Lights fade to black-out

SCENE 3

To open: General exterior lighting

Cue 3:   The music gets louder   (Page 14)
             Lights fade to black-out

SCENE 4

To open: General interior lighting

Cue 4:   They dance for a while   (Page 16)
             Lights fade to black-out

SCENE 5

To open: General exterior lighting

Cue 5:   The two are frozen in a pose   (Page 19)
          Lights fade to black-out

                         Scene 6

To open: General interior lighting

Cue 6:   They both exit   (Page 20)
          Lights fade to black-out

                         Scene 7

To open: General exterior lighting

No cues

                         Scene 8

Cue 7:   THE END appears on the title device   (Page 23)
          Black-out

EFFECTS PLOT

Cue 11   **Mr Kane**: "Just not the adventurous type, I suppose!"   (Page 17)
           Sound of a camera clicking several times

Cue 12   **Kathleen**: "No, I mean I'd really love to."   (Page 18)
           Series of camera clicks

Cue 13   **Kathleen**: "But sure what on earth for?"   (Page 19)
           Sound of a camera rewinding

SONG SUGGESTIONS

It's You, It's You, It's You by Joe Dolan (Irish Singer/Songwriter)
A waltz by Strauss
The Typewriter by Percy Grainger
"Nessun Dorma" from *Turandot* by Puccini
"The Stars Were Shining" from *Tosca* by Puccini
"Love Duet" from Act 1 *Madam Butterfly* by Puccini
"One Fine Day" from *Madam Butterly* by Puccini
"What is Life" from *Orfeo* by Gluck
Clarinet Concerto 2nd movement Mozart
In a Persian Market by Ketelbey
Eine Kleine Nacht Muzik by Mozart

Printed by The Kingfisher Press, London NW10 7AS